a Prayerbook *for* Catechumens

Alison Berger

TWENTY-THIRD PUBLICATIONS
A Division of Bayard MYSTIC, CT 06355

Twenty-Third Publications
A Division of Bayard
185 Willow Street
P.O. Box 180
Mystic, CT 06355
(860) 536-2611
(800) 321-0411
www.twentythirdpublications.com

ISBN:1-58595-147-1
Library of Congress Catalog Card Number: 2001131979
Printed in the U.S.A.

Contents

Orientation

My mother once found my niece Vicki kneeling near a statue of Mary in the front window of my parents' living room. Mom asked, "Vicki, what are you doing?"

"I'm praying, Grandma," the four-year-old replied. Vicki had had no formal introduction to prayer. Yet it came to her very naturally.

In many ways prayer is like the air we breathe. We can try to explain it, but to grasp how vital it is to us we have to experience it.

You bring to this book and to the RCIA process your own experience of prayer. Whatever religious background you come from, you have probably prayed on some occasion or other, perhaps without realizing you were praying.

A Prayerbook for Catechumens will help you unlock some of the riches of the Catholic tradition of prayer. You'll find it a rich and varied tradition, with many different expressions of prayer. Each of the prayer experiences in this book focuses on a different form of prayer or a different aspect of your faith life. You can celebrate these prayer experiences with your sponsor and other catechumens, or use them for personal reflection and prayer. You'll probably discover some elements that are already familiar to you, and others that are new. You may feel more comfortable with some prayer expressions than with others, and that is perfectly normal. You are encouraged to make this book as helpful and effective as possible for yourself by adapting and using the material to meet your own spiritual needs.

A Prayerbook for Catechumens includes three sections of prayers: prayer experiences centered on the liturgy (taken in its broadest sense) and the Word of God; prayer experiences based on the rites and rituals of the RCIA process; and personal prayer, including devotional prayer and a treasury of basic prayers.

Your Prayer Environment

For personal prayer, it's helpful to set aside a "quiet corner" and time where you won't be easily distracted or interrupted. Some visible symbols in your "corner" can help establish a prayerful atmosphere: a lighted candle (symbol of Christ's presence), a copy of the Bible, a cross or crucifix, a religious picture or nature scene, reflective music. Place yourself in a comfortable position. Relax and focus by breathing deeply several times. Put aside other concerns during your prayer time.

Breaking Open the Word:
Praying with Scripture and the Saints

Scripture is God's word and as such has a wonderful power to transform our lives and attitudes. Each chapter of this book includes a brief Scripture quote related to the focus of that chapter. I recommend that you read the entire passage from your Bible, if possible. Read it through slowly and thoughtfully once. Then go back and note any words or phrases that especially struck you. Focus on these and on their meaning for you at this moment of your life. What might God be saying to you through these words? Let your feelings and thoughts rise to God in prayer. This form of praying Scripture will help you apply God's Word to your daily life in a very personal way. It engages you more fully than a mere intellectual reflection would.

You might use the same process with the passages from the saints. Their writings can be considered a practical as well as mystical reflection on Scripture and on the teachings of the Church. The saints' lives and their writings are part of our Catholic tradition.

Breaking Open the Experiences: Journaling

Journaling is an aid to prayer and spiritual growth. Writing down our thoughts and feelings helps us become more aware of God's action in our daily lives. Our experiences take on a different dimension when we try to express them in writing or drawing, and we can find new or hidden meaning in them.

Some people prefer to use a diary style journal with dates and days of the week, but any type of notebook can be used for journaling. Date your entry. If you're writing in the evening, you might want to briefly describe some of the events and ideas that had special significance for you that day. If you're journaling in the morning, you may want to put down some thoughts about the day ahead, or reflect on the previous day. As you write, reflect: where is God present in all this? Do I sense that God is leading me in a certain direction?

A Prayerbook for Catechumens is intended to be a handbook for you as you walk with your sponsor and RCIA group in preparation for the sacraments of initiation, and as you continue to progress in your life of faith. Hopefully the prayerbook will remind you of God's great love for you, of God's presence in your life, and of your call to a unique relationship with God.

A blessed journey!

PART I

The Liturgy

In the New Testament the word liturgy refers not only to the celebration of divine worship but also to the proclamation of the Gospel and to active charity. In all of these situations it is a question of the service of God and neighbor .(Catechism of the Catholic Church, *#1070)*

The liturgy of the Church involves each of us fully in prayer, in catechesis, and in transformation into Christ. All Christian prayer finds its source in the liturgy. Catechesis, along with reflection on the visible signs of the liturgy, leads us into the mystery of Christ. Through the liturgy we learn to center our life in Christ, and Christ lives and acts in us. We celebrate the liturgy as a community, but each of us brings something unique to that celebration.

Use these prayer experiences as often as you wish during your RCIA journey, in your own prayer times, with your sponsor, with your RCIA group.

CHAPTER 1

Praying with the Christian Community

The whole community celebrates the liturgy, each person according to his or her own role. "Faith is a treasure of life which is enriched by being shared" (*Catechism*, #949).

Opening Prayer

> Lord Jesus, let me share in the fruits of the Spirit:
> love, joy, peace, patience, kindness, generosity,
> faithfulness, gentleness, and self-control. May I
> be guided by the Spirit in my relationship with
> others, bearing with the burdens of others so as
> to fulfill the law of Christ.

Based on Galatians 5:22—6:2

Breaking Open the Word

Read and absorb these words from Scripture and the saints. Let them help you formulate some type of resolve or response to the message of the prayer experience.

The Word of God

Awe came upon everyone, because many wonders and signs were being done by the apostles. All who believed were together and had all things in common; they would sell their possessions and goods and distribute their proceeds to all, as any had need. Day by day, they broke bread at home and ate their food with glad and generous hearts, praising God and having the good will of all the people.

Acts 2:43–47

From Christian Witnesses

Be faithful, then, in following the example of Jesus; be strong and firm in faith, and love the community as you love one another. Remain united in the truth and be as gentle as the Lord in dealing with one another, looking down on no one. If you can do good, do not hesitate for charity frees us from death. Be submissive to one another, and let your behavior among unbelievers be beyond reproach.

St. Polycarp, letter to the Philippians

Breaking Open the Experience

Use these reflections, questions, and exercises as a spring-board for prayer and sharing.

A Concert of Lives

Many years ago I had a very powerful experience of what it means to be a community of faith. The closing liturgy for the International Eucharistic Congress, held in Philadelphia, was being celebrated in an outdoor stadium. The assembly was made up of Catholics from all over the world. When the time came for the Profession of Faith, we all sang the Creed in Latin. There was a great, swelling concert of voices—people of many different cultures and conditions of life sharing and proclaiming the same beliefs.

It's hard to describe what the experience was like—it was similar to what you feel when you hear exquisite music or read a great piece of literature. The beauty and truth of it touches the depths of your soul.

- Can you remember a moment when you had a powerful experience of community (in your family, among friends, in praying with others)? Write what you remember about it: circumstances, feelings, consequences, and so on. What made it such a powerful experience?

- Read and reflect on Paul's description of the Church as the body of Christ in 1 Corinthians 12:12–31.

What does it tell you about how we should relate to one another?

- What is your experience of the community of faith in the celebration of the Word? In your relationship with other catechumens, with your sponsor, with other members of the parish family?
- How well do you participate in the community? In prayer and in works?

Closing Prayer

Praise the Lord! I will give thanks to the Lord with my whole heart, in the company of the upright. Great are the works of the Lord, studied by all who delight in them. He has shown his people the power of his works, in giving them the heritage of the nations. He sent redemption to his people; he has commanded his covenant forever. Holy and awesome is his name.

Psalm 111: 1–2, 6, 9

CHAPTER 2

Celebration of the Word

The gospel passage from Luke that speaks of the encounter of the disciples from Emmaus with the risen Christ, gives us insight into the sharing of the Word. Jesus walked with the disciples, explaining the Scriptures to them. Then he sat at table with them, "took bread, blessed and broke it and gave it to them" (Lk 24:13–35).

Like the disciples and like Mary, who treasured the word of the Lord in her heart, you are invited to listen to God's Word with mind and heart, then reflect on it and apply it to your lives as you break open the Scriptures with your RCIA group.

Opening Prayer

Loving God, help me to hear your Word with an open heart and to live it with faith in you.

Breaking Open the Word

*Read and absorb these words from Scripture and the saints.
Let them help you formulate some type of resolve or response
to the message of the prayer experience.*

The Word of God

When anyone hears the word of the kingdom and
does not understand it, the evil one comes and
snatches away what is sown in the heart; this is
what was sown on the path….But as for what was
sown on good soil, this is the one who hears the
word and understands it, who indeed bears fruit
and yields, in one case a hundredfold, in another
sixty, and in another thirty.

Matthew 13:19–23

From Christian Witnesses

While Mary contemplated everything she had read
and heard, she grew even more in faith, wisdom,
and charity. The mysteries of God were opened up
to her, and joy filled her heart. Her mind was
entirely blessed because, through the presence and
action of the Spirit, she was always open to the
power of God's word.

Do as Mary did. Look deep into your heart so you
can be cleansed from your sins. Whether we con-
template the greatness of God or serve the needs of

our neighbors by good works, we do all this through the love of Christ. We offer God our spiritual purification not in temples made by man but in the recesses of the heart where Jesus freely enters.

St. Lawrence Justinian,
sermon on the purification of the Blessed Virgin Mary

Breaking Open the Experience

Use these reflections, questions, and exercises as a springboard for prayer and sharing.

Listening with the Heart

The first time I took part in a group meditation on Scripture, I was really nervous. I spent much of the time trying to come up with a brilliant reflection on the passage we were meditating on. But after I went to several of these group sessions, I began to realize that I was so busy listening to myself that I wasn't really listening to God.

A true sharing of God's word on the deepest level calls for humility and trust. It means recognizing and accepting our limitations and those of other people, while being open to conversion, to having our lives turned around, gradually transformed by God's love. Sharing in a group takes effort and practice, but it bears fruit in profound moments of faith-sharing.

- With whom do you share confidences, secrets, dreams? Why is it easier to speak of these with some persons than with others?

- What part does listening play in sharing? What do you think it means to "listen with the heart"? What qualities do we need to truly listen to God and to one another?

- Did you find it difficult at first to take part in breaking open the Scriptures? Has it become easier for you? What has made it easier?

- What have you learned from sharing the word of God with others? How has it changed your life?

Closing Prayer

How sweet are your words to my taste, sweeter than honey to my mouth! Through your precepts I get understanding; therefore I hate every false way. Your word is a lamp to my feet and a light to my path.

Psalm 119:103–105

CHAPTER 3

The Liturgy of the Hours

The Liturgy of the Hours marks each hour of the day with prayer and reading of the Scriptures, so that the "whole course of the day and night is made holy by the praise of God" *(Sacred Constitution on the Liturgy, #84)*. Each member of the Church takes part according to their situation in life and their calling.

The Prayer of the Hours centers around the psalms, and includes hymns, litanies, and prayers that celebrate the time of day, the liturgical season, and the feast or saint of the day. The reading from the Word of God, readings from the Fathers of the Church, the saints and spiritual masters "reveal more deeply the meaning of the mystery being celebrated, assist in understanding the psalms, and prepare for silent prayer"*(Catechism, #1177)*.

In this chapter, you will find a prayer experience modeled after Evening Prayer in the Liturgy of the Hours.

God, come to my assistance.
—Lord, make haste to help me.
Glory to the Father,
and to the Son,

and to the Holy Spirit,
as it was in the beginning, is now,
and will be forever. Amen.

Hymn

At the name of Jesus
Ev'ry knee shall bow,
Ev'ry tongue confess him
King of glory now;
'Tis the Father's pleasure,
We should call him Lord,
Who from the beginning
Was the mighty Word.

Psalm 16

Protect me, O God, for in you I take refuge.
I say to the Lord, "You are my Lord;
I have no good apart from you."
The Lord is my chosen portion and my cup;
you hold my lot.
The boundary lines have fallen for me
in pleasant places;
I have a goodly heritage.
I bless the Lord who gives me counsel;
in the night also my heart instructs me.
I keep the Lord always before me; because he is
at my right hand, I shall not be moved.

Psalm-prayer

Lord Jesus, my heart is glad and my soul rejoices
in you. You show me the path of life. In your presence there is fullness of joy forever.

Canticle: Philippians 2:6–11

Though he was in the form of God,
Jesus did not regard equality with God as something to be exploited,
But emptied himself,
taking the form of a slave,
being born in human likeness.
And being found in human form,
he humbled himself
And became obedient to the point of death—
even death on a cross.
Therefore God also highly exalted him
and gave him the name
that is above every name,
so that at the name of Jesus
every knee should bend,
in heaven and on earth and under the earth,
and every tongue should confess
that Jesus Christ is Lord,
to the glory of God the Father.

Reading: Colossians 1:2–6

Grace to you and peace from God our Father. In our prayers for you we always thank God, the Father of our Lord Jesus Christ, for we have heard of your faith in Christ Jesus and of the love that you have for all the saints, because of the hope laid up for you in heaven. You have heard of this hope before in the word of truth, the gospel that has come to you.

Canticle of Mary: Luke 1:46–49

My soul magnifies the Lord,
and my spirit rejoices in God my Savior,
for he has looked with favor
on the lowliness of his servant.
Surely, from now on all generations will call me blessed;
for the Mighty One has done great things for me,
and holy is his name.

Prayer

Merciful God, may I love you above all things, and reach the joy that you have promised to all who walk in the footsteps of your Son, our Lord Jesus Christ. Amen.

CHAPTER 4

Praying the Church Seasons

In the course of the liturgical year the Church unfolds the whole mystery of Christ. By recalling the mysteries of our redemption, she makes the riches of the Lord's merits accessible to all the faithful.

Opening Prayer

Bless the Lord, all rain and dew; sing praise to him and highly exalt him forever.
Bless the Lord, all you winds; sing praise to him and highly exalt him forever.
Bless the Lord, winter cold and summer heat; sing praise to him
and highly exalt him forever.
Bless the Lord, nights and days;
sing praise to him and highly exalt him forever.

Breaking Open the Word

Read and absorb these words from Scripture and the saints.
Let them help you formulate some type of resolve or response
to the message of the prayer experience.

The Word of God

For everything there is a season, and a time for
every matter under heaven: a time to plant, and a
time to pluck up what is planted; a time to kill,
and a time to heal; a time to weep, and a time to
laugh; a time for war, and a time for peace.

Ecclesiastes 3:1–8

From Christian Witnesses

Heaven and earth and everything within them
call to me to love you....What is the object of
my love? I asked the earth and it replied, "Not
I." I asked everything in the world, and they
said the same thing. I asked the oceans, the
creeping creatures, and they replied, "We are
not your God; look further." I asked the wind
and the air and they said, "I am not God." I
asked the sun, the moon, and the stars, and
they replied, "We are not the God you are looking for." I said to all of them, If you are not
God, tell me something about him. And they
cried out with one voice: "He made us." My

question was in my gazing on them, and their reply was in their beauty.

St. Augustine, Confessions, Book X, #8–9.

Breaking Open the Experience

Use these reflections, questions, and exercises as a springboard for prayer and sharing.

Seasons of Faith

One of the things I love most about living in New England is the change of seasons. The blazing colors of autumn; the cold and stark beauty of winter; the lavish burst of new life in spring....These familiar seasons that are part of the book of nature send messages about the passage of time in the rhythm of my life.

The seasons of the Church year are part of the book of faith. Through them we celebrate the events and teachings of Jesus' life—not merely as past events but as mysteries that have transformed human history and continue to transform our lives. The liturgical year centers around the resurrection of Jesus at Easter, begins and continues with the events leading up to the passion and death of Jesus. After Easter the Church continues to celebrate the effects of the resurrection in the life of Christians, right from the early Church.

• Which is your favorite season of the year? Why?

- What does the Advent season mean to you? Christmas? Lent? What preoccupies you most during each of these seasons?
- Discuss with your sponsor and RCIA group how to celebrate these seasons more fruitfully.
- Ask your sponsor about the rich customs associated with the Church seasons.

Closing Prayer

Here are two meal prayers that you can use, one for Advent and one for Lent.

Advent

Loving God, we rejoice at the coming of your Son Jesus. Help us to prepare for his coming with hearts full of faith and love. Bless us and the food we are about to share, in his name.

Lent

God of love and mercy, lead us through the penance and purification of Lent to the joy of Easter. May we show our love for you by our loving service to one another. Grant this in Jesus' name. Amen.

CHAPTER 5

Praying about Christian Service

One of the vital aspects of liturgy is active charity, service to others. We are called to live out our love for God and our neighbor, not just talk about it.

Opening Prayer

Loving God, let the word of faith which you have spoken to me through Scripture and through other people bear fruit in works of love and service.

Breaking Open the Word

Read and absorb these words from Scripture and the saints. Let them help you formulate some type of resolve or response to the message of the prayer experience.

The Word of God

One who sows sparingly will also reap sparingly, and the one who sows bountifully will also reap bountifully. Each of you must give as you have made up your mind, not reluctantly or under compulsion, for God loves a cheerful giver.

2 Corinthians 9:6–8

From Christian Witnesses

St. Martin de Porres treated his brothers in community with the deep love that comes from faith and humility. He loved everyone because he saw them as children of God and as brothers and sisters in Christ. He would overlook the faults of others because he believed his sins deserved more punishment than anyone else's. He tried to persuade the criminal to reform; he comforted the sick; he provided food and clothing for the poor. Throughout the countryside the people called him "Martin the charitable."

Pope John XXIII,
homily at the canonization of St. Martin de Porres

Breaking Open the Experience

Use these reflections, questions, and exercises as a springboard for prayer and sharing.

Service in the Details

For some of us the term "Christian service" or "active charity" might call to mind the heroic lives of persons like Mother Teresa of Calcutta who spent her life caring for the poorest of God's children. Another is Blessed Damien de Veuster of Molokai, who chose to live among the lepers, to serve them and to minister to them, aware that eventually he would contract the disease.

Not all of us are called to serve our neighbor in the same way these two holy people did. But our days can still be filled with acts of service to others: showing respect to each person we contact; being patient and compassionate; helping someone in difficulty; caring for a sick child or spouse; calling or visiting a lonely neighbor or family member. And we can extend these acts of service further by bringing and/or serving food at a food pantry; ministering to persons in a nursing home or in prison; taking an active interest in social justice issues, and in movements and organizations that aim to benefit the needy (e.g., Habitat for Humanity, Catholic Relief Services, Catholic Campaign for Human Development).

- Make a list of all your activities of the past two days. Be as detailed and specific as you can. Don't over-look even the most routine actions (such as a phone call or waking the kids for school or putting tools away). How many opportunities did you have for serving God in serving others?
- How can you bring the ideal of Christian service into your daily life more concretely?
- Discuss with your sponsor and/or RCIA group some forms of Christian service and ministry that you might take part in. Discern with them whether you are ready at this point.

Closing Prayer

God has created me to do him
some definite service.
He has committed some work to me
which he has not committed to another.
I have my mission,
I may never know it in this life,
but I shall be told it in the next....
I shall do good—I shall do his word.
I shall be an angel of peace.

John Henry Cardinal Newman

CHAPTER 6

Bringing Catechesis to Prayer

During your catechumenate you are learning, sharing, and living the faith of the Church: through celebrations of the Word; celebration of the rites and rituals belonging to the catechumenate and to the period of purification and enlightenment; the example of members of the faith community; your conversations with your sponsor. Bringing what you learn and experience to prayer will enrich your prayer and your faith life, and will help you make the faith more fully your own.

Opening Prayer

Glory to the Father and to the Son and to the Holy Spirit, as it was in the beginning, is now, and will be forever. Amen.

Breaking Open the Word

Read and absorb these words from Scripture and the saints. Let them help you formulate some type of resolve or response to the message of the prayer experience.

The Word of God

Do not store up for yourselves treasures on earth, where moth and rust consume and where thieves break in and steal; but store up for yourselves treasures in heaven, where neither moth nor rust consumes and where thieves do not break in and steal. For where your treasure is, there your heart will be also.

Matthew 6:19–21

From Christian Witnesses

Although I know well, Margaret, that because of my past wickedness I deserve to be abandoned by God, I can only trust in God's merciful goodness. His grace has strengthened me until now and made me content to lose goods, land, and life as well, rather than to swear against my conscience. I will not mistrust him, Meg, though I shall feel myself weakening and on the verge of being overcome with fear. I shall remember how Saint Peter at a blast of wind began to sink because of his lack of faith, and I shall do as he did: call upon Christ and pray to him for help. And, Margaret, I know this well: that without my fault God will not let me be lost. I shall, therefore, with good hope commit myself wholly to him.

St. Thomas More,
a letter written in prison to his daughter Margaret

Breaking Open the Experience

Use these reflections, questions, and exercises as a springboard for prayer and sharing.

- Choose a topic that came up in one of your recent celebrations of the Word or in a discussion with your sponsor. It might be a truth or an experience that is difficult for you to accept or grasp. Think about what it means to your life, to your growth in faith.

- Make an act of faith in God. Talk to God about the difficulty you are having with this truth/experience. Or talk to God about the joy or inspiration you feel in learning and experiencing this aspect of Christian faith.

- Read Jesus' conversation with Nicodemus (John 3:1–21) or with his disciples after his discourse on the Bread of life (John 6:52–71), which tell of the struggle Jesus' own followers had in accepting what they heard and saw. Or read chapter 1 or chapters 3–4 of Paul's letter to the Philippians, in which he urges them to rejoice in Christ.

Closing Prayer

My God, I believe in you, I hope in you, I love you with all my heart.

PART II

Celebrating
the Journey

First Acceptance
of the Gospel

The Rite

Your acceptance into the Order of Catechumens begins
with a greeting, a dialogue in which you declare what
you are seeking from the Church. Then you celebrate
your first acceptance of the gospel.

Opening Prayer

Loving God, you have brought me this far. Be
with me and the other catechumens step by
step. Help me be faithful to this journey toward
eternal life.

Breaking Open the Word

Read and absorb these words from Scripture and the saints.
Let them help you formulate some type of resolve or response
to the message of the prayer experience.

The Word of God

Everyone then who hears these words of mine and
acts on them will be like a wise man who built his
house on rock. The rain fell, the floods came, and
the winds blew and beat on that house, but it did
not fall because it had been founded on rock

Matthew 7:24–25

From Christian Witnesses

O immeasurably tender love! You, my God, are an
infinite well of love; it seems you love us so much
that you could not live without us. Yet you are our
God and have no need of us. What could move
you to be so merciful? Neither duty nor any need
you have of us—but only love!

St. Catherine of Siena, The Dialogue

Breaking Open the Experience

Use these reflections, questions, and exercises as a spring-
board for prayer and sharing.

I Love You Forever

I know a four-year-old named Eric who has a favorite book about a mother and her child. Whenever the child in the story asks: "Mother, how long will you love me?" the mother responds, "I love you forever." Eric's mom reads part of the story to him every night. As she reads, she looks at her little boy; tears come to her eyes and she cannot finish the story. As she tucks Eric in for the night, she whispers, "I love you forever." It has gradually become a special ritual for both of them. When Eric is away from his mom for a night, he calls. At the end of their "good nights" he'll hint, "Mom, what about the story?" "I love you forever," she answers.

What a message that story holds for Eric and his mother! And what about the message the mother and son give each other?

The part of the Rite called the First Acceptance of the Gospel tells us that God truly speaks to everyone. God sends God's message of love and truth and wisdom in many ways: through creation, through other people, through events, through Scripture—but especially through his Son Jesus. We are called to walk in the light of Christ and trust in his wisdom, so we may come to believe in him and love him with all our heart.

- Jot down some words that are meaningful for you, that you like the sound of, that evoke happiness, peace, love. If words don't work for you, try pictures.

What colors do you like? What subjects do you like (portraits, still life, landscapes, religious themes)? Or music: what kind of music do you prefer?

- Look at the words or pictures or music you chose. What might they tell you about yourself, as you are now?

- Think over the past twenty-four hours, the past week. What words of love and of truth did you hear? When and how? From whom? Perhaps they were not all pleasant to hear. Write down some of these words. Do you find a message from God in any of them? Talk to God about it.

- In Scripture God tells us over and over: "I love you forever." Read any of the parables in chapter 15 of the gospel of Luke. Does any particular phrase or saying strike you? Stay with that phrase. What do you think God is saying to you at this moment in that passage?

Closing Prayer

Lord Jesus, thank you for the gift of the gospel. Help me listen to your word with my heart as well as my mind, and put it into practice by loving God and my neighbor.

CHAPTER 2

Signing with the Cross

The Rite

As you are received into the catechumenate, your forehead and senses are signed with the cross. The celebrant prays that you may receive this sign and follow in Christ's footsteps.

Opening Prayer

Loving God, you call me to share a life of love
and hope in Christ. May I treasure his cross as a
sign of that new life. Help me to be a sign of his
love: in my words and actions, at home, at work,
at prayer.

Breaking Open the Word

Read and absorb these words from Scripture and the saints.
Let them help you formulate some type of resolve or response
to the message of the prayer experience.

The Word of God

Jesus said: "Do not fear. Only believe, and [your daughter] will be saved."

Luke 8:50

From Christian Witnesses

We are celebrating the feast of the cross which drove away darkness and brought in the light. As we keep this feast, we are lifted up with the crucified Christ, leaving behind earth and sin so that we may gain the things above. Rightly could I call this treasure (the cross) the fairest of all fair things and the costliest, for on it and through it and for its sake the riches of salvation that had been lost were restored to us.

St. Andrew of Crete,
sermon on the feast of the Holy Cross

Breaking Open the Experience

Use these reflections, questions, and exercises as a spring-board for prayer and sharing.

A Sign of Faith

For as far back as I can remember, certain practices in our home were as much a part of our daily ritual as getting out of bed in the morning. One such ritual was the good-night kiss. No matter how busy or tired our parents were, or who might be visiting, we never omitted lining up or waiting in bed for that final greeting of the day. It was a powerful, visible sign of our parents' love, of our family unity, and of their wish that we have a blessed sleep.

Many parents bless their children with the sign of the cross at night. They are asking God to watch over and protect their child, to show God's love. Signing with the cross is an expression of their faith and love. The sign of the cross is the sign of our new way of life in Christ. With this sign of his love, Christ strengthens us for our journey. He calls us to know and follow him, together with our sisters and brothers in the community of faith.

- What are some simple rituals that are part of your family's experience, of your own life (for example, gathering for a special meal or celebration)? What effect have these had on you, on your personal growth, on your attitudes toward yourself, others, life?

- Is there a particular action or gesture that gives you peace or touches your heart (the smile of a child, a walk in the woods, a needy person's blessing)?

- Recall your experience of the signing with the cross: on your forehead...on your ears...on your eyes...on your lips...over your heart...on your shoulders...on your hands...on your feet. What did you think of and feel during the signing? What did the signing mean to you? Share your experience with your sponsor and/or RCIA group.

- Read about Jesus raising the official's daughter to life (Lk 8:49–56). Notice the details, Jesus' gestures and words, and the response of the people. Do any particular phrases strike you more than others? Write down what this passage means to you. Compose a prayer based on this passage.

Closing Prayer

Make the sign of the cross on your senses as you say these prayer petitions:

(ears) May I hear your voice, Lord.

(eyes) May I see your glory.

(lips) May I respond to your Word.

(heart) May Christ live in me by faith.

CHAPTER 3

Minor Exorcisms

The Rite

The minor exorcisms are one of the rites belonging to the catechumenate. They point to the struggle and self-denial that are part of the Christian life, and to the need for God's help.

Opening Prayer

Loving God, help me to look into my heart, to recognize my sins and weaknesses, and to ask your forgiveness. Heal me; protect me from the spirit of evil, so I may become the temple of your Holy Spirit.

Breaking Open the Word

Read and absorb these words from Scripture and the saints. Let them help you formulate some type of resolve or response to the message of the prayer experience.

The Word of God

The people who sat in darkness have seen a great light, and for those who sat in the region and shadow of death light has dawned.

Matthew 4:16, quoting Isaiah

From Christian Witnesses

Let me know you, O Lord, as you know me; let me know you as I am known. Power of my soul, enter into my heart and make it fit for you, so you may possess it without spot or wrinkle. For you love truth, and whoever lives by the truth walks in the light. What can I hide from you, whose eyes see into the depths of my conscience, even if I would not confess my faults? When I recognize my sins, you become more beloved and longed for. May I be ashamed of myself and renounce my sins and choose you.

St. Augustine, Confessions

Breaking Open the Experience

Use these reflections, questions, and exercises as a springboard for prayer and sharing.

Naming the Darkness

You may have read the story of little Sadako, who lived with her family in the city of Hiroshima, Japan. When the atomic bomb was dropped on the city, Sadako's whole family was killed. Sadako herself was badly burned. While she was in the hospital, she realized that she didn't have long to live.

Instead of letting revenge or hatred take hold in her heart, this young girl decided, "This can never again happen to people. Each day I'm going to make a white crane out of paper. I will send it to someone and ask them to be a peacemaker."

Sadako did just that every day for 683 days, until she died. Other people, inspired by her example, started making the cranes and sending them. These white cranes still tell people that life can be better if we live in peace. Each of us makes a difference, starting with our own lives.

In the prayers called the minor exorcisms we recognize the reality of sin, and ask God to bring light and life to clear away the darkness. We pray for God's help in the struggle that forms part of every Christian's commitment to follow Jesus.

- Can you recall a recent painful moment—a disagreement or estrangement or loss of trust? Was peace restored? How? If not, what could you do to restore it?

- Read the front page of today's newspaper or a news article in a magazine. Can you find at least one story that contains an element of darkness—sin or suffering? Is there anything you can do about the situation? What?

- What are the areas of darkness in my life where I need to let God bring light and healing? In my attitudes, in my actions, in what I say (or don't say)?

- How can I help bring peace and healing to my family? To my neighborhood? To my workplace? Discuss this with your sponsor.

Closing Prayer

Make a list of some of the weaknesses you have noted in yourself. As you say the following prayer, burn the list as a sign of your openness to God's healing love.

God of mercy, please burn away all the weakness
and sinfulness in me with the fire of your love.
Help me grow in faith, in hope, and in love for
you and for all my brothers and sisters.

CHAPTER 4

Blessings

The Rite

The blessings are bestowed during your catechumenate so that you may receive from the Church courage, joy, and peace on your journey.

Opening Prayer

God of peace, may I come to know and love you and obey your will with a generous heart. I ask this through Jesus your Son.

Breaking Open the Word

Read and absorb these words from Scripture and the saints.
Let them help you formulate some type of resolve or response
to the message of the prayer experience.

The Word of God

Then Jesus took [the children] up in his arms, laid
his hands on them, and blessed them.

Mark 10:13–16

From Christian Witnesses

"The kingdom of God is within you." This teaches
us that those who purify their hearts of every created thing and every evil desire will see the image
of God in the beauty of their own souls. When
you are told that the majesty of God is exalted
above the heavens, that his glory is inexpressible,
his beauty indescribable, and his nature infinitely
above our own, do not despair because you cannot behold the object of your desire. If by a dili-
gent life of virtue you wash away the film of dirt
that covers your heart, then the divine beauty will
shine forth in you.

St. Gregory of Nyssa, on the Beatitudes

Breaking Open the Experience

Use these reflections, questions, and exercises as a spring-board for prayer and sharing.

Signs of Love

One summer a friend and I were doing some missionary work in Appalachia. We were so impressed by the faith of the folks we met during our visits there. Amid the poverty and hardships they faced, their main comfort was their belief in God's presence and care for them.

I remember one elderly man in particular. He lived in a broken-down trailer with very little furniture and no electricity. As we stood outside chatting and offered him a copy of the Bible, he suddenly raised his hand to his lips. "Listen!" We followed his gaze to look at the tall pines that were swaying in the wind.

"When I feel lonely or blue, I listen to God's voice speaking to me—in the trees, in the sky. I know he cares about me. That's what matters."

The blessings that are given to you during your cate-chumenate are a sign of God's love and the care of the faith community you are joining. In these prayers we recognize that God is present and active in our lives, and we thank God for all his gifts.

• Take a few minutes to reflect on the blessings in your life—the big ones as well as the small ones. Make a list on decorated paper and frame it, if you wish. Say a prayer of thanks to God, and to the people who bring God's blessings to you.

- Reflect on the most recent blessing prayer said for you as a catechumen. What did you experience during the rite? What did the words mean to you?

- There are nine prayers of blessing that can be used for this rite. All of them are meaningful expressions of faith and caring. The next time one of these blessings is prayed, write down or ask for a copy of the words. Reflect on them, and discuss the meaning with your sponsor and/or other catechumens.

- Write your own prayer of blessing. Write a group prayer of blessing.

Closing Prayer

If possible offer this prayer of blessing with your RCIA group or family. Gather around a table and join hands. If you have a Bible, place it on the table as a sign of God's presence among you.

Loving God, thank you for all your gifts. Bless our family with love and peace. Give us the help we need to put your Word into practice in our lives. (Offer a prayer for each member of the family, or invite them to pray for one another.)

CHAPTER 5

Anointing

The Rite

Another rite belonging to the catechumenate, the rite of anointing with oil symbolizes the need for God's help and strength in professing and persevering in the faith.

Opening Prayer

Jesus, you spoke words of spiritual freedom and forgiveness to your people. Open my ears and heart to your word now. Help me to believe in you, and to show that belief in action.

Breaking Open the Word

Read and absorb these words from Scripture and the saints. Let them help you formulate some type of resolve or response to the message of the prayer experience.

The Word of God

The God of all grace, who has called you to his eternal glory in Christ, will himself restore, support, strengthen and establish you.

1 Peter 5:10

From Christian Witnesses

Where can the weak find a place of firm security and peace, except in the wounds of the Savior? Indeed the more secure my place there, the more he can help me. Through these sacred wounds we can see the secret of his heart, the great mystery of love, the sincerity of his mercy with which he visited us from on high. More mercy than this no one has than that he lay down his life for those who are doomed to death.

St. Bernard of Clairvaux, sermon on the Song of Songs

Breaking Open the Experience

Use these reflections, questions, and exercises as a springboard for prayer and sharing.

Signs of Healing and Strength

I once had the privilege of being present for the celebration of the ordination of a bishop. The whole celebration was filled with symbolism but what impressed me most was the rite of anointing. It reminded me of the important role oil played in biblical times. Kings, prophets, and priests were consecrated with oil; it was a sign of their being set apart by God for their particular role.

Anointing with oil is part of the rite of four sacraments: baptism, confirmation, holy orders, and anointing of the sick. Anointing is a sign of healing but also of consecration and strength. It symbolizes the seal of the Holy Spirit, who guides us in living out our commitment to follow Jesus in serving others, in witnessing to God's loving presence, and in worshiping and praising God.

- What use do we make of different kinds of oil (cooking oil, rubbing oil, motor oil, bath oil, etc.)? What effect does the oil have in each case?

- Have you ever participated in a celebration/ritual where someone was anointed? What was the occasion? What did the anointing symbolize?

- Read and reflect on the anointing of David in 1 Samuel 16:1–13. What did the anointing mean? How did it affect David's life?

- Reflect on the first time you were anointed as a catechumen. What was the setting? Do you recall the Scripture readings? What did you think and feel as you were anointed? Talk to God about all this. Share your reflections with others in your group.

- After reflecting on your experience, write down one or two things you learned from it that you can carry with you as you continue your journey toward baptism.

- If someone you know is ill, visit them and pray with them for God's healing in body and spirit.

Closing Prayer

The oil of anointing usually has a light, sweet natural odor. If you have lightly scented bath oil, cologne, or perfume, use it to remind you of God's healing presence.

Jesus, you took my sins upon your own body
and were nailed to the cross, so that I might die
to sin and live in holiness. Give me the strength
to profess my faith in you each day.

CHAPTER 6

A Pause in the Journey

A Day of Discernment

Throughout the catechumenate but especially as you draw near the time for the Rite of Election, you will want to set aside some quiet time to discern your readiness for the Easter sacraments. This discernment is also done in discussions with your sponsor and the RCIA team.

As you begin this day, set aside some time in a quiet space to read, reflect, and pray.

Opening Prayer

God of mystery, you have called me to this journey of faith. Help me look honestly and without fear at my experience this far. Help me and those guiding me to know if I'm ready for the commitment of faith at baptism.

Breaking Open the Word

Read and absorb these words from Scripture and the saints.
Let them help you formulate some type of resolve or response
to the message of the prayer experience.

The Word of God

As God's chosen ones, holy and beloved, clothe
yourselves with compassion, kindness, humility,
meekness, and patience. Bear with one another
and, if anyone has a complaint against another,
forgive each other; just as the Lord has forgiven
you, so you also must forgive. Above all, clothe
yourselves with love.

Colossians 3:12–14

From Christian Witnesses

Lord, shed upon our darkened souls the brilliant
light of your wisdom so that we may be enlightened and serve you with renewed purity. Sunrise
marks the hour for us to begin our toil, but in our
souls, Lord, prepare a dwelling for the day that
will never end. Grant that we may come to know
the risen life and that nothing may distract us
from the delights you offer.

St. Ephrem

Breaking Open the Experience

Use these reflections, questions, and exercises as a spring-board for prayer and sharing.

A Pause in the Journey

When I need to make an important decision, I usually try to clarify my objective, weigh the pros and cons of each course of action open to me, seek the advice of others, and take some time for reflection before coming to a conclusion. In discerning your readiness to celebrate the sacraments you will rely on two other means: prayer and awareness of the "clues" God gives you each day as to where you are on your journey. What is God saying to your heart: through events, through other people, through your experiences?

Here are four ways that will help in discernment: prayer, silence, consulting spiritual persons, some form of journaling.

- What were some of your hopes, fears, and expectations when you were accepted into the catechumenate? Have any of these been resolved/fulfilled? Have any of them changed? How and why?

- Ask God's help in looking honestly at your spiritual journey so far: outstanding moments, moments of doubt, moments of deeper understanding, and so on. Note these moments in your journal. Do you see a pattern? Talk to God about it.

Following are the criteria the Rite offers for discerning your readiness for the Easter sacraments. Spend a few moments in silence asking God for guidance.

- *Conversion in mind and in action.* Have I tried to let the Word of God influence my thinking and actions? Some particular areas: prayer, forgiveness, justice, trust, service to others.

- *Spirit of faith and charity.* Am I developing a habit of prayer, of turning to God with confidence and trust? Have I grown in kindness, understanding, patience, giving? In my capacity to receive love?

- *Acknowledged intention to receive the sacraments.* Am I ready to make the commitment that comes with the gift of salvation in Christ? Do I feel at home in the faith community? Do I desire to contribute to the growth of this community?

Closing Prayer

Lord God, thank you for your goodness to me. Help me to know you and to know myself, to recognize and listen to your voice in the words and actions of other people, in what I experience, in what I truly desire. Show me the way you want me to follow.

CHAPTER 7

The Rite of Sending

The Rite

At the conclusion of the period of the catechumenate, a rite of sending may be celebrated. This rite offers the local faith community the opportunity to express its approval of the catechumens and to assure them of the community's care and support.

Opening Prayer

Jesus Lord, may I share in the life of my parish community, the joys as well as the sorrows. Free me from selfishness and teach me to put others first.

Breaking Open the Word

Read and absorb these words from Scripture and the saints. Let them help you formulate some type of resolve or response to the message of the prayer experience.

The Word of God

Then Jesus summoned his twelve disciples and gave them authority over unclean spirits...and to cure every disease and every sickness. These twelve Jesus sent out with the following instructions: As you go proclaim the good news, "The kingdom of heaven has come near."

Matthew 10:1,5,7

From Christian Witnesses

The Church is called Catholic or universal because it has spread throughout the entire world, from one end of the earth to the other....It is most aptly called church, which means an "assembly" of those called out, because it "calls out" all people and gathers them together. The word "assemble" is used for the first time in the Bible when God chooses Aaron to be high priest. Christian churches are already multiplying all over the world. The psalm can be applied to them: Sing a new song to the Lord, let the assembly of the saints sing his praises.

St. Cyril of Jerusalem, catechetical instruction

Breaking Open the Experience

Use these reflections, questions, and exercises as a spring-board for prayer and sharing.

A Community Send-Off

The year I left home to go to a private high school in Boston, my parents gave a big party. Relatives whom I hadn't seen for years came to wish me well. Friends and family provided useful gifts to take with me. I experienced an extra-strong sense of family support that day.

The Rite of Sending is your "send-off" celebration. The community gathers to affirm, support, and bless you with the gifts of their prayers and encouragement. Your parish community will continue to play an important role in your faith development both before and after the Rite of Initiation.

- Have you ever been to a "sending-off" party: before a voyage, when a child was leaving for school or college, etc.? What was the feeling of community like at that event? How was that send-off like a ritual?

- What is your experience of community (family, neighborhood, work place, parish)? Are there any adjustments you need to make in your attitude, understanding, or life in order to be more comfortable with community? To participate more fully in community? Talk to God about it. Ask your sponsor for suggestions.

- What was your experience of the Rite of Sending? the presentation? affirmation by the godparents and assembly? the intercessions prayer? Did one part in particular impress you?
- What meaning does this sending have for your future?

Closing Prayer

Compose your own prayer of thanksgiving for the blessings you have received through your parish community.

CHAPTER 8

The Rite of Election

The Rite

The Rite of Election is the second step in Christian initiation. It usually coincides with the beginning of Lent.

Opening Prayer

Lord God, thank you for your goodness. Bless me as I enter into the next stage of Christian initiation. Increase my trust in your grace and guidance.

Breaking Open the Word

Read and absorb these words from Scripture and the saints. Let them help you formulate some type of resolve or response to the message of the prayer experience.

The Word of God

But now thus says the Lord, he who created you, O Jacob, he who formed you, O Israel: Do not fear, for I have redeemed you; I have called you by name, you are mine. When you pass through the waters, I will be with you; and through the rivers, they shall not overwhelm you....For I am the Lord, your God, the Holy One of Israel, your Savior.

Isaiah 43:1–4

From Christian Witnesses

In the gospel of John the Lord says: In this will all men know that you are my disciples, if you have love for each other.... We should therefore examine our hearts and form a true judgment on our attitudes of mind and heart. If we find the fruit of love in our hearts, we must not doubt God's presence there. If we desire to increase our ability to welcome this great Guest, we should be even more generous, persevering in charity. Any time is the right time for doing good but these days of Lent are of special encouragement. If we want to celebrate the Lord's paschal mystery in holiness of mind and body, we should ask for this grace, because charity contains all the other virtues and covers a multitude of sins.

St. Leo the Great

Breaking Open the Experience

Use these reflections, questions, and exercises as a springboard for prayer and sharing.

What's in a Name?

When Mary Magdalene met Jesus on Easter morning, she did not recognize him until he called her name, "Mary!" In speaking her name he revealed himself to her, and at the same time called her to a new relationship.

Mary responded, "Rabbuoni," which means teacher. It was an act of faith, of love, of commitment—all expressed in a name.

The Rite of Election focuses on the mystery of God's presence and action in your life. By offering your name for enrollment you make a response of faith to God's invitation to a covenant relationship.

- How often during the week do you sign your name as a sign of your approval or agreement to something?
- Read Matthew 16:13–20, in which Jesus gives Simon a new name. Why do you think Jesus did that?

- Take some moments of silence to reflect on your experience of the Rite of Election: the presentation of the catechumens; affirmation by the godparents and assembly; invitation and enrollment of names; act of admission or election; intercessions for the elect; prayer over the elect.
- Write down your impressions. Hear God speaking to you through your experience. Has it given you any new insight into your journey? Share your reflections with others.

Closing Prayer

Loving God, during this lenten journey may I
grow in charity and be constant in prayer. May I
dedicate my daily work as an offering to you.

CHAPTER 9

The First Scrutiny

The Rite

The period of Purification and Enlightenment focuses on purification, redemption, and conversion. The scrutinies are meant to discover and heal whatever is sinful and weak in the elect, and to recognize and strengthen what is good.

Opening Prayer

Holy Spirit, you search every heart. Help me to see my weaknesses and to overcome them through your power.

Breaking Open the Word

Read and absorb these words from Scripture and the saints. Let them help you formulate some type of resolve or response to the message of the prayer experience.

The Word of God

On the last day of the festival, the great day, while Jesus was standing there, he cried out, "Let anyone who is thirsty come to me, and let the one who believes in me drink."

John 7:37–38

From Christian Witnesses

A Samaritan woman came to draw water: Jesus said to her: Give me water to drink….She was astonished that a Jew should ask her for a drink of water. But the one who was asking for a drink of water was thirsting for her faith. He asks for a drink, and he promises a drink. He is in need, as one hoping to receive, yet he is rich as one about to satisfy the thirst of others. He says: If you knew the gift of God….But he is still using veiled language as he speaks to the woman and gradually enters into her heart. What is this living water he will give if not the water spoken of in Scripture? He was promising the Holy Spirit in satisfying abundance.

St. Augustine, a treatise on John

Breaking Open the Experience

Use these reflections, questions, and exercises as a spring-board for prayer and sharing.

Living Water

"The water that I shall give him will become in him a fountain of living water, welling up into eternal life." This is a new kind of water, a living, leaping water, surging up for those who are thirsty.

But why did Jesus call the grace of the Spirit "water"? Because all things are dependent on water; plants and animals have their origin in water. Water comes down from heaven as rain and brings about many different effects. In a like manner the Holy Spirit gives grace to each person just as the Spirit wills. Just as a dry tree puts out shoots when it is watered, so does the person bear the fruit of holiness when through repentance that person is made worthy of receiving the Holy Spirit.

St. Cyril of Jerusalem, catechesis on the Holy Spirit

- Reflect on the experience of thirst. What do you feel when you are truly thirsty? What spiritual gifts do you "thirst" for?

- God bestows on each of us gifts of nature and grace. Which of your gifts helps you on your spiritual journey? What gifts do you see in your sponsor? In other catechumens? In other members of the faith community? Pray that these gifts be strengthened.

- What hinders you from satisfying your thirst (weaknesses, sin, e.g., unwillingness to forgive, insensitivity to the needs of others)?
- Water is one of the major sacramental symbols of our faith. Read and reflect on what you wrote in response to the first two questions. Does what you wrote take on a new meaning in light of the First Scrutiny? Write about what you felt during that experience.

Closing Prayer

If possible, celebrate this rite with your sponsor, group, or family. You will need a glass bowl, cups, and a pitcher of water. Invite each member of the group to pour a cup of water into the glass bowl. Then invite them one by one to dip their hands into the water and bless themselves, as you recite this prayer.

Loving God, every day you give us new life in so many ways. Your gift of water cleanses and strengthens us. May this water remind us of your call to follow you, to cleanse ourselves of whatever keeps us from loving you more. Bless us now through this water. Amen.

CHAPTER 10

The Creed

The Rite

The presentation of the Creed, which expresses the heart of the Church's faith, is meant to fill you with the sure light of faith.

Opening Prayer

God of goodness, thank you for entrusting to me the words of faith in the Creed. May I receive them each day with a sincere heart, and be faithful to them.

Breaking Open the Word

Read and absorb these words from Scripture and the saints. Let them help you formulate some type of resolve or response to the message of the prayer experience.

The Word of God

When Jesus' disciples heard his words, they said, "This teaching is difficult; who can accept it?" Because of this many of his disciples turned back and no longer went about with him. So Jesus asked the twelve, "Do you also wish to go away?" Simon Peter answered him, "Lord, to whom can we go? You have the words of eternal life."

John 6:60, 66–68

From Christian Witnesses

The Church received the faith from the apostles and their disciples and preserves it carefully. With one soul and one heart, the Church professes this faith, preaches and teaches it the same everywhere, as though with a single voice. For though there are different languages, there is only one tradition.

St. Irenaeus, Against Heresies

Breaking Open the Experience

Use these reflections, questions, and exercises as a springboard for prayer and sharing.

I Believe

The movie *A Man for All Seasons* powerfully portrays the struggle between the faith of St. Thomas More and the passion of his king. In one scene Sir Thomas tries to explain to his friend the Duke of Norfolk why he has resigned as Lord Chancellor of England. When the Duke asks Thomas why he has given up his office and all its privileges for a belief, Sir Thomas replies: "What is important is that I believe it...no, that *I* believe."

St. Thomas' faith was not something that he donned on Sunday. It filled his life. He viewed everything else through the lens of his faith.

In the Creed you receive a centuries-old summary of the Catholic faith. You inherit it from and share it with saints and sinners of every age in history.

- When did you last express your belief and trust in someone—with words, or a gesture, or a look? Expressing our belief strengthens it. Why do you think that is true?

- Write a list of the persons, truths, and things you believe in. Offer this list to God in prayer.

- Reflect on your experience of the presentation of the Creed: the readings; the presentation; the prayers.

What did you think and feel? What did God say to your heart?

- Is there one particular part of the Creed that impresses you more? That means more to you? Why? You might choose to repeat that part frequently as a prayer.

Closing Prayer

Loving God, I believe that you are one God,
Father, Son, and Holy Spirit. I believe that your
Son Jesus Christ took our human nature, died to
redeem us, and rose again. I believe these and all
the truths you have revealed because you are
Truth.

CHAPTER 11

The Second Scrutiny

The Rite

The second scrutiny focuses on Christ the light of the world. Christ's light enables us to see God's love and the barriers that prevent this love from transforming us.

Opening Prayer

Jesus, you are the light of the world and the light of my life. May I follow you so I do not walk in darkness.

Breaking Open the Word

Read and absorb these words from Scripture and the saints. Let them help you formulate some type of resolve or response to the message of the prayer experience.

The Word of God

In the beginning was the Word, and the Word was with God, and the Word was God....What has come into being in him was life, and the life was the light of all people. The light shines in the darkness, and the darkness did not overcome it.

John 1:1–5

From Christian Witnesses

You know that no one can walk in the way of truth without the light of truth which comes from me, the true Light, through the gift of understanding. You must also have the light of faith which I give you in holy baptism, unless you put it out through sin. In baptism, through the blood of my Son you received the virtue of faith. If you exercise this faith with the light of reason, reason will in turn be enlightened by faith. This faith will give you life and lead you along the path of truth. With this light you will reach me, the true light.

The Lord speaking to St. Catherine of Siena, The Dialogue

Breaking Open the Experience

Use these reflections, questions, and exercises as a spring-board for prayer and sharing.

Light of the World

Anne Sullivan, who taught Helen Keller how to "see," was concerned above all that the darkness young Helen lived in would also keep her mind and soul in darkness. So she did all she could to give Helen a different kind of sight.

The gospel passage for this scrutiny is full of imagery. Jesus focuses on sight and light, on healing and the difficulties of recovery. The blind man's problems were not over when his sight (both physical and spiritual) was restored. Because he clung to his belief that Jesus had cured him and therefore must be from God, he was expelled by the religious leaders. Jesus became his light and the center of his belief.

- Close your eyes and try to imagine what it would be like to live with blindness. What would be most difficult for you? What would you miss most?

- There are other, worse kinds of blindness. What are some of the other forms of blindness that we might suffer from?

- Light is necessary not only for sight but for life itself. What are some effects light has on living beings—for example, plants?

- Did the celebration of the Second Scrutiny help you to understand sight and light in a new way? How?
- Where do you experience darkness or blindness in your life? What obstacles keep you from seeing, from being in the light?
- What do you need for your sight to be restored? What are some of the risks that such a recovery might involve for you?
- Write your own spontaneous prayer for sight, asking Jesus our light to heal the darkness in your life.

Closing Prayer

Who are you, sweet light that fills me and illumines the darkness of my heart? You guide me like a mother's hand, and if you let me go, I could not take another step. You are the space that surrounds and contains my being.

St. Edith Stein, from Edith Stein: Selected Writings

CHAPTER 12

The Third Scrutiny

The Rite

The period of Purification and Enlightenment continues with reflection on Christ, the resurrection and the
life.

Opening Prayer

Lord, I believe that you are the Messiah, the Son
of God, and that whoever lives and believes in
you will never die.

Breaking Open the Word

Read and absorb these words from Scripture and the saints. Let them help you formulate some type of resolve or response to the message of the prayer experience.

The Word of God

Beloved, let us love one another, because love is from God; everyone who loves is born of God and knows God. Whoever does not love does not know God, for God is love.

1 John 4:7–8

From Christian Witnesses

If Christ dwells in us as our friend and leader, then we can bear all things, for he will help us, strengthen us, and never abandon us. Jesus is a true friend. If we desire to please God and be filled with his graces, these graces must come to us from Jesus' hands, through his most sacred humanity.... What more do we desire from such a good friend? Unlike other friends, Jesus will never abandon us when we are troubled or sad. Happy the one who truly loves Jesus and remains at his side.

St. Teresa of Avila, Autobiography

Breaking Open the Experience

Use these reflections, questions, and exercises as a springboard for prayer and sharing.

Resurrection

Do you remember the story of Heidi, the little orphan who goes to live with her grandfather—an embittered recluse—and brings him back to life through her gift of love?

God's love—shown to us in Jesus—brings us to life, renews us. And when we love as God loves us, as St. Augustine says, we become new persons. "This love is the gift of the Lord who said, 'As I have loved you, you also must love one another.' His object in loving, then, was to enable us to love each other."

- Have you ever experienced good resulting from a difficult, even painful, situation? Reflect on and pray over that experience in your heart.

- What "little deaths"—weaknesses, losses, limitations—have been part of your life? Ask God to bring new life out of these little deaths.

- Reflect on your own experience of the Third Scrutiny: the readings and homily, the intercessions, exorcism, and prayers. What signs of new life did you find or feel? Share these with your sponsor and/or group.

- Reread the passage from John 11:1–45. What signs of loss or fear or doubt can you find? What signs of love and trust? Which prevailed, death or life?
- Into what area of your life does God's love need to enter more fully? Let a prayer for this love rise from your heart. Pray also for those who do not know God's love.

Closing Prayer

Praise to your unbounded love, Jesus! Moved to pity by my misery, you offer me so many means of growing in love for you. You are all mine, Jesus. Your heart, too, is mine because you have given it to me so often. But your heart is filled with light. Mine is filled with darkness. Let me pass from this darkness into your light and life.

St. Gemma Galgani

CHAPTER 13

Presentation of the Our Father

The Rite

The presentation of the Our Father is celebrated during the week following the Third Scrutiny. This prayer, a key to all other prayers, gives us a deeper understanding of the spirit of adoption by which we call God Father and Mother.

Opening Prayer

Loving God, may I always treasure your love
which allows me to call you Father and Mother.
Help me to live as your son/daughter.

Breaking Open the Word

Read and absorb these words from Scripture and the saints. Let them help you formulate some type of resolve or response to the message of the prayer experience.

The Word of God

Ask, and it will be given to you; search, and you will find; knock, and the door will be opened for you. If you know how to give good gifts to your children, how much more will your Father in heaven give good things to those who ask him!

Matthew 7:7, 11

From Christian Witnesses

How merciful is the Lord, full of compassion and kindness. He invited us to call God our Father and in turn to be called true children of God. Not one of us would ever have dared to use this name unless Jesus himself had taught us to. Therefore, my dear friends, when we call God our Father we should act as God's children. If we are happy to call God Father, may God also be pleased to call us God's children. We are temples of God; let us live accordingly. Nothing that we say or do should be unworthy of the Spirit.

St. Cyprian, on the Lord's Prayer

Breaking Open the Experience

Use these reflections, questions, and exercises as a spring-board for prayer and sharing.

Summary of the Gospel

Have you ever tuned an instrument? Or heard an orchestra warming up? The musical scale is the guide, the model, so to speak, for making sure the sound of each instrument is pure and in harmony with the others.

The Our Father is the prayer by which we keep our own prayers "in tune." Its petitions are a model for ours. This prayer which Jesus himself taught us is "the summary of the whole gospel" (*Catechism, #2761*).

- Do you have any favorite prayers among those you have learned? Why are they your favorites?

- What do you think are the most important things to pray for?

- What was your experience of the presentation of the Our Father: the Liturgy of the Word, the presentation, the prayers? What new meaning did it give to your praying of the Our Father?

- Pray the Our Father slowly, as a group or by yourself. Are there one or two phrases of the Our Father that seem to touch you, speak to your heart, more at this moment in your life?

Closing Prayer

My God, well may I cling to you—for whom do I have in heaven but you? And who upon earth besides you, my heart and my portion forever?

St. Elizabeth Ann Seton

CHAPTER 14

Preparation Rites on Holy Saturday

The Rite

Holy Saturday should be a day of prayer and reflection in preparation for the celebration of the sacraments at the Easter Vigil.

Opening Prayer

The Lord is my shepherd, I shall not want. He makes me lie down in green pastures; he leads me beside still waters; he restores my soul.

You prepare a table before me in the presence of my enemies; you anoint my head with oil; my cup overflows.

Surely goodness and mercy shall follow me all the days of my life, and I shall dwell in the house of the Lord my whole life long

Psalm 23:1–3, 5–6

Breaking Open the Word

Read and absorb these words from Scripture and the saints. Let them help you formulate some type of resolve or response to the message of the prayer experience.

The Word of God

Looking up to heaven, Jesus sighed and said to the deaf man, "Ephphatha," that is, "Be opened." And immediately his ears were opened, his tongue was released, and he spoke plainly.

Mark 7:31–36

From Christian Witnesses

The Apostle Paul tells us to rejoice, but in the Lord, not in the world. Just as a person cannot serve two masters, so we cannot rejoice both in the world and in the Lord. So let joy in the Lord take place over all other joy, until joy in worldly things is no more. Let your joy in the Lord increase daily, and your joy in worldly things decrease. This does not mean we are not to rejoice in this life, rather, we are to find joy in this life as well as in the next. Just because we are in the world does not mean that we are not in the Lord. If God is everywhere, then isn't God always with us?

St. Augustine of Hippo, from a sermon

Breaking Open the Experience

Use these reflections, questions, and exercises as a springboard for prayer and sharing.

The Face of Christ

One newly baptized young woman shared with her sponsor the wonderful experience of her baptism during the Easter Vigil. "As the priest poured the water and said the words, 'I baptize you,' I looked into the water in the font. I saw the reflection of my face and of the Easter candle. And I was struck most powerfully by the thought: I am being baptized into Christ, into the life of Christ. I felt such joy and awe, such humility and thankfulness at that moment!"

- Spend some time in thanksgiving to God for having accompanied you on this journey.
- Remind yourself of the reasons why you decided to follow the call to be baptized.
- Pray for the grace to be faithful to the commitment you are making.
- If your parish celebrated the preparation rites, reflect now on your experience of them: the reading, the recitation of the Creed, the Ephphatha Rite.
- In the Ephphatha Rite the priest touches your lips and ears, and prays that you may profess the faith you hear. What are some ways that you can profess that faith after your baptism?

Closing Prayer

I praise you, I glorify you, I bless you, O my God, for the wonderful blessings you have lavished on me, even though I am unworthy of them.
I bless your clemency in waiting for me, your sweetness in correcting me, your tenderness in calling me, your mercy in pardoning me, your goodness in filling me with favors, your compassion in protecting me, and your truth in rewarding me. How can I speak of your infinite goodness? For when I flee from you, you call me back. When I return, you receive me; when I stumble, you raise me up. When I despair, you fill me with joy.... I cannot praise you enough for all your goodness. But I thank you, and ask that you increase your life in me, preserve that life, and bring me to eternal life with you. Amen.

St. Thomas Aquinas

CHAPTER 15

Celebration of the Sacraments of Initiation

The Rite

During the Easter Vigil all the powerful symbols you experienced, in different ways, during your time of preparation come together in the celebration of the sacraments, initiating you into a new life.

Opening Prayer

Loving God, may I celebrate with a grateful heart the gift of new life in your Son Jesus Christ, and show its effects in the way I live.

Breaking Open the Word

Read and absorb these words from Scripture and the saints. Let them help you formulate some type of resolve or response to the message of the prayer experience.

The Word of God

I pray that the God of our Lord Jesus Christ, the Father of glory, may give you a spirit of wisdom and revelation as you come to know him, so that, with the eyes of your heart enlightened, you may know what is the hope to which he has called you, what are the riches of his glorious inheritance among the saints, and what is the immeasurable greatness of his power for us who believe.

Ephesians 1:17–19

From Christian Witnesses

When I look at the mystical body of the Church, I cannot recognize myself in any of the roles which St. Paul describes. Besides, I want to share in the good works of the whole body. Love seemed to me to be the center of my vocation. I know that the Church has a heart, and that this heart is on fire with love. I know that the same love spurs all the members to action...that love sets the boundaries for all vocations, that love is everything, that love embraces every time and place. And so in my joy I exclaimed, Jesus, my love, at last I have found my vocation, and that vocation is love. In the heart of my mother the Church I shall be love.

St. Thérèse of Lisieux

Breaking Open the Experience

Use these reflections, questions, and exercises as a spring-board for prayer and sharing.

Born Again!

You were brought to the baptismal font just as Christ was taken down from the cross and placed in the tomb. Each of you was asked, "Do you believe in the name of the Father and of the Son and of the Holy Spirit?" You made the profession of faith that brings salvation, then you were immersed in the water and three times rose again. This is a symbol of the three days Christ spent in the tomb. When you were immersed in the water, it was as though night had fallen and you could not see in the darkness. But when you came out of the water, it was like coming into the light of day. At that moment you died and were born again. This is an amazing thing! We did not actually die and rise; we only did this symbolically. But we have truly been saved....How boundless is Christ's love!

Mystagogy, from the Jerusalem Catechesis

- Reflect prayerfully on your experience of the celebration of the sacraments.

  Celebration of baptism: the presentation; the litany of the saints; the blessing of the water; the renunciation of sin and profession of faith; the baptism; clothing and presentation of the candle.

  Celebration of confirmation: invitation; laying on of hands; anointing.

  Celebration of the Eucharist.

- Reflect on the sacramental symbols of water, bread, and oil. How are these especially meaningful to you in your life right now? How can you carry out their symbolism in your work, in your relationships with others, in your service to the poor and needy? (You'll be reflecting on this symbolism throughout the period of Mystagogy.)

Closing Prayer

Loving God, let me pray with St. Thérèse: In the heart of the Church I shall be love. No matter what kind of work I do, no matter what my situation in life, I can grow close to you through love, a love that is lived out in the details of daily life. Holy Spirit, fill me with this love. Amen.

PART III

Personal Prayer

1. Prayers of Devotion

Holy Hours

Originally the Eucharist was reserved in a home or church so that, after the celebration of Mass, the sick could receive the body of Christ. Gradually through the centuries it became a common practice to spend time in prayer and adoration before the Eucharist reserved in tabernacles in the churches. The practice of the Holy Hour or Hour of Adoration became even more popular with the spread of devotion to the Sacred Heart of Jesus.

The Holy Hour as an extension of the liturgy can be an important part of a person's spiritual life. Reading and reflecting on Scripture, praying the Liturgy of the Hours and other prayers, discernment of one's relationship with God are some means of spiritual growth often practiced during a Holy Hour.

Nine First Fridays

The practice of the nine first Fridays developed from a private revelation of Jesus to St. Margaret Mary Alacoque. Among other messages that Jesus entrusted to Margaret Mary, he encouraged faithful Catholics to receive Communion on the first Friday of every month and to spend time in prayer on the first Thursday, in remembrance of his passion.

Mary

We honor Mary of Nazareth as the mother of Jesus Christ, the Son of God, and as the model of the perfect disciple. Mary's faith and love in responding to God's call are praised in the gospel: "Blessed are you among women....Blessed is she who believed that there would be a fulfillment of what was spoken to her by the Lord" (Lk 1:42, 45).

It certainly did require both faith and love on Mary's part to hold fast to God's word as she saw her son rejected, opposed, jeered at, and finally led to crucifixion. But there were also the daily, smaller tests of faith, of struggling to understand what God was asking of her. Mary, Joseph, and Jesus were poor; did Mary sometimes long to give better things to her son? What must it have been like to live in a neighborhood where her son was not accepted, in fact, where his own townspeople tried to throw him over a cliff? When Jesus was away preaching, how did Mary cope with loneliness? And anxiety?

The Church celebrates Mary's faith and asks for her intercession with many different prayers. The most well-known prayer practices are the Angelus and the rosary.

The Angelus

The Angelus has been used for centuries to mark and sanctify the day, especially by persons who could not read the prayers of the Office. The church bells would ring and people would stop whatever they were doing to pray together or alone. The Angelus centers around God's invitation to Mary to become the mother of his Son, and Mary's yes (see p. 102).

The Rosary

The rosary developed during the Middle Ages as a popular substitute for the Liturgy of the Hours. It combines prayer with meditation on the main events (mysteries) in the life of Jesus and Mary. There are three sets of mysteries: the joyful mysteries, the sorrowful mysteries, and the glorious mysteries. The prayers include the Apostles Creed, the Our Father, the Hail Mary, and the Glory Be (see p. 105).

Feasts of Mary

Several feasts honoring Mary are celebrated during the Church year. Three of the major feasts are also holy-days of obligation in the United States (which means they are celebrated like Sundays): the Solemnity of Mary Mother of God, the Immaculate Conception of Mary (which celebrates Mary conceived without sin), and the Assumption (which honors Mary's privilege of being taken into heaven body and soul).

The Saints

We also celebrate God's holiness as it shines in the example of outstanding Christian witnesses. In every age there have been persons recognized for their lives of faithfulness to the gospel and their practice of faith, hope, and charity to an heroic degree. We honor these friends of God and ask them to intercede for us with their prayers. Many of the saints are included in the Church's liturgical calendar. Many more are not listed there but may still be honored and imitated.

The Way of the Cross

The Way (or Stations) of the Cross is a popular lenten devotion in parish churches. During the eleventh to thirteenth centuries countless pilgrims went to the Holy Land to walk in the footsteps of Jesus on his way to Calvary. Later, when pilgrimages were no longer safe or practical, the Stations of the Cross became a popular outdoor devotion. In the 1700s the stations were often celebrated inside churches and eventually figures representing the stations became a familiar feature in Catholic churches. The Way of the Cross includes spoken prayers and meditation on the stations. It can be prayed by individuals, although most often it is a group prayer (see p. 106).

2. Basic Prayers

Sign of the Cross

In the name of the Father and of the Son and of the Holy Spirit. Amen.

Our Father

Our Father, who art in heaven, hallowed be thy name. Thy kingdom come, thy will be done on earth as it is in heaven. Give us this day our daily bread, and forgive us our trespasses as we forgive those who trespass against us. And lead us not into temptation, but deliver us from evil. Amen.

Hail Mary

Hail Mary, full of grace, the Lord is with you. Blessed are you among women, and blessed is the fruit of your womb, Jesus. Holy Mary, mother of God, pray for us sinners, now and at the hour of our death. Amen.

The Apostles Creed

I believe in God, the Father almighty, creator of heaven and earth.

I believe in Jesus Christ, his only Son, our Lord, who was conceived by the Holy Spirit, born of the Virgin Mary, suffered under Pontius Pilate, was crucified, died, and was buried. He descended to the dead. On the third day he rose again. He ascended into heaven and sits at the right hand of God, the Father almighty. From thence he shall come to judge the living and the dead. I believe in the Holy Spirit, the holy Catholic Church, the communion of saints, the forgiveness of sin, the resurrection of the body, and life everlasting. Amen.

Glory Be

Glory be to the Father, and to the Son, and to the Holy Spirit, as it was in the beginning, is now, and ever shall be. Amen.

An Act of Faith

My God, I firmly believe that you are one God in three divine Persons, Father, Son, and Holy Spirit. I believe that your divine Son became man and died for our sins, and that he will come to judge the living and the dead. I believe these and all the truths which the Catholic Church teaches, because you have revealed them, who can neither deceive nor be deceived.

An Act of Hope

My God, relying on your infinite goodness and promises, I hope to obtain pardon of my sins, the help of your grace, and life everlasting, through the merits of Jesus Christ, my Lord and Redeemer.

An Act of Love

My God, I love you above all things, with my whole heart and soul, because you are all good and worthy of all love. I love my neighbor as myself for love of you. I forgive all who have injured me, and I ask pardon of all whom I have injured.

An Act of Sorrow

Dear God, I am truly sorry for the wrong things I have done. And for the good things I should have done but didn't. I'm sorry because sin separates me from you and from your love. With your help I resolve not to sin again, and to avoid whatever could lead to sin.

Prayer to the Holy Spirit

Come, Holy Spirit, fill the hearts of your faithful and enkindle in them the fire of your love. Send forth your Spirit and they shall be created, and you shall renew the face of the earth.

Let us pray: O God, who filled the hearts of your faithful with the light of the Holy Spirit, grant that, by the coming of the same Holy Spirit, we may be truly wise and ever rejoice in his consolation. Through Christ our Lord. Amen.

Hail Holy Queen

Hail, holy Queen, Mother of mercy, our life, our sweetness, and our hope. To you do we cry, poor banished children of Eve. To you do we send up our sighs, mourning and weeping in this valley of tears. Turn then, most gracious advocate, your eyes of mercy toward us. And after this our exile show us the blessed fruit of your womb, Jesus. O clement, O loving, O sweet Virgin Mary.

Prayer of St. Bernard (Memorare)

Remember, O most gracious Virgin Mary, that never was it known that anyone who fled to your protection or sought your help was left unaided. Inspired by this confidence I turn to you, O Virgin of virgins, my Mother. To you I come, before you I stand, sinful and sorrowful. O Mother of the Word Incarnate, despise not my petitions but in your mercy hear and answer me. Amen.

The Angelus

The angel of the Lord declared unto Mary
And she conceived of the Holy Spirit.

Hail Mary, etc.

Behold the handmaid of the Lord
May it be done to me according to your word.

Hail Mary, etc.

And the Word was made flesh
And dwelt among us.

Hail Mary, etc.

Pray for us, holy Mother of God,
That we may be made worthy
of the promises of Christ.

Let us pray: O Lord, it was through the message of an angel that we learned of the incarnation of your Son Christ. Pour your grace into our hearts, that by his passion and cross we may be brought to the glory of his resurrection. Through the same Christ our Lord. Amen.

Prayer to My Guardian Angel

Angel of God, my guardian dear,
    to whom God's love entrusts me here,
Ever this day be at my side,
    to light and guard, to rule and guide.
Amen.

Mantras

Mantras are short prayers repeated often throughout the day.

- Jesus, son of the living God, have mercy on me, a sinner.
- Jesus, make me love you more and more.
- My God, I believe in you, I hope in you, I love you with all my heart.
- Blessed be God. Blessed be God's holy name.
- Virgin Mary, mother of Jesus, pray that I may become more and more like your Son Jesus.
- St. Joseph, foster father of Jesus and husband of Mary, pray for us and for the dying of this day.
- Lord, send good laborers into your harvest.

Prayer before Meals

- Bless us, O Lord, and these your gifts, which we are about to receive from your bounty. Through Christ our Lord. Amen.
- Bless us, Lord, bless this food and those who have prepared it. Bless those who share it with us (names). May we always remember those who are in need. Amen.

Prayer after Meals

We give you thanks, loving Father, for these and all your gifts, you who live and reign forever and ever. Amen.

Prayer of St. Francis of Assisi

Lord, make me an instrument of your peace.
Where there is hatred, let me sow love;
   where there is injury, pardon;
   where there is doubt, faith;
   where there is despair, hope;
   where there is darkness, light;
   and where there is sadness, joy.
O divine Master,
   grant that I may not so much seek
   to be consoled, as to console;
   to be understood, as to understand;
   to be loved, as to love.
For it is in giving that we receive;
   in pardoning that we are pardoned;
   and in dying that we are born to eternal life.

Prayer of St. Patrick

Christ be with me, Christ before me,
   Christ behind me,
Christ within me, Christ beneath me,
   Christ above me,
Christ on my right, Christ on my left,
Christ where I lie, Christ where I sit,
   Christ where I rise,
Christ in the heart of everyone who thinks of me,
Christ in every eye that sees me,

Christ in every ear that hears me.

May your salvation be ever with us, O Lord.

The Mysteries of the Rosary

The Joyful Mysteries

1. The angel announces to Mary the birth of Jesus (Lk 1:26–33)
2. Mary visits St. Elizabeth (Lk 1:39–42)
3. Jesus is born in Bethlehem (Lk 2:1–7)
4. Mary and Joseph present Jesus in the Temple (Lk 2:22–24)
5. Jesus is found among the teachers in the Temple (Lk 2:41–47)

The Sorrowful Mysteries

1. Jesus prays in the Garden of Gethsemane (Lk 22:39–42)
2. Jesus is tied to a pillar and beaten (Jn 19:1)
3. Jesus is crowned with thorns (Mt 27:27–31)
4. Jesus carries his cross (Jn 19:16–17)
5. Jesus dies on the cross (Lk 23:46)

The Glorious Mysteries

1. Jesus rises from the dead (Lk 24:1–6)
2. Jesus is taken up to heaven (Acts 1:6–11)
3. The Holy Spirit comes to the apostles (Acts 2:1–4)
4. Mary is taken up into heaven (Song 2:10–13)
5. Mary is crowned as Queen (Rev 12:1)

The Way of the Cross

R. *We adore you, O Christ, and we bless you,*
because by your holy cross you have redeemed the world.

The First Station
Jesus is condemned to death (Mt 27:26)
We adore you, O Christ, etc.

The Second Station
Jesus carries his cross (Jn 19:16–17)
We adore you, O Christ, etc.

The Third Station
Jesus falls under his cross (Is 53:7)
We adore you, O Christ, etc.

The Fourth Station
Jesus meets his mother (Jn 19:26–27)
We adore you, O Christ, etc.

The Fifth Station
Simon helps Jesus carry his cross (Mt 27:32)
We adore you, O Christ, etc.

The Sixth Station
Veronica wipes the face of Jesus (Lk 23:27)
We adore you, O Christ, etc.

The Seventh Station
Jesus falls the second time (Is 50:5–6)
We adore you, O Christ, etc.

The Eighth Station

Jesus meets the women of Jerusalem (Lk 23:28)

We adore you, O Christ, etc.

The Ninth Station

Jesus falls the third time (Is 50:7)

We adore you, O Christ, etc.

The Tenth Station

Jesus is stripped of his clothing (Jn 19:23)

We adore you, O Christ, etc.

The Eleventh Station

Jesus is nailed to the cross (Lk 23:33)

We adore you, O Christ, etc.

The Twelfth Station

Jesus dies on the cross (Lk 23:46)

We adore you, O Christ, etc.

The Thirteenth Station

Jesus is taken down from the cross (Lk 23:52–53)

We adore you, O Christ, etc.

The Fourteenth Station

Jesus is placed in the tomb (Jn 19:39–42)

We adore you, O Christ, etc.

Of Related Interest...

A Prayerbook for Volunteers
Deborah McCann

In this realistic, down-to-earth and humorous look at the important work of volunteers, the author offers heartfelt prayers and reflections on the various aspects of this "unsung" ministry. Both the upside and the downside of the volunteer's role is beautifully expressed here and the experiences of volunteers are related to those of Jesus.

1-58595-139-0, 48 pp, $5.95 (J-93)

A Prayerbook for Catechists
Gwen Costello

Drawing on her own experience as catechist and DRE, this popular author offers prayers from the heart for a variety of seasons and situations. Each prayer reflects a firm belief in God's loving care for catechists and students, in the uniqueness of each child, and in the importance of the catechist's vocation.

0-89622-979-3, 48 pp, $5.95 (J-26)

A Teacher's Prayerbook
To Know and Love Your Students
Ginger Farry

Prayer poems for and about students are followed by brief reflections or questions for teachers to ponder in relation to their own students; others chronicle the good and bad days, the joys and disappointments in the life of a teacher.

0-89622-727-8, 64 pp, $4.95 (M-89)

A Single Mother's Prayerbook
Ginger Farry

Here are the prayers of a single mom who called upon God in child-rearing situations as well as in times of loneliness and frustration. Through them the reader learns that we are never alone and that God is always present.

0-89622-973-4, 64 pp, $7.95 (J-17)

Available at religious bookstores or from:

TWENTY-THIRD PUBLICATIONS
A Division of Bayard PO BOX 180 • MYSTIC, CT 06355
1-800-321-0411 • FAX: 1-800-572-0788 • E-MAIL: ttpubs@aol.com
www.twentythirdpublications.com
Call for a free catalog